Love Your Tropical Fish

Piranha

Tetras

Love Your Tropical Fish

Don Harper

W. Foulsham & Co. Ltd.
London • New York • Toronto • Cape Town • Sydney

W. Foulsham & Company Limited
Yeovil Road, Slough, Berkshire, SL1 4JH

ISBN 0-572-01388-4

Copyright © 1986 W. Foulsham & Co. Ltd.

All rights reserved.
The Copyright Act (1956) prohibits (subject to certain very limited exceptions) the making of copies of any copyright work or of a substantial part of such a work, including the making of copies by photocopying or similar process. Written permission to make a copy or copies must therefore normally be obtained from the publisher in advance. It is advisable also to consult the publisher if in any doubt as to the legality of any copying which is to be undertaken.

Printed in Spain by Cayfosa, Barcelona.
Dep. Leg. B-27227-1986

Contents

	Introduction	7
1	Choosing Your Fish	12
2	Housing	45
3	General Management	53
4	Breeding	57
5	Health	59
6	Shows and Societies	64

Introduction

The keeping of tropical fish is a relatively new hobby, which has captivated millions of people around the world in a comparatively short space of time. A number of factors have been responsible for the rapid development of this pastime. In the first instance, air transportation meant that fish could be flown long distances, to arrive at their destinations in good health. Then as such fish were kept and studied, their breeding habits become better understood, and today, a high percentage of the fish offered for sale are bred on special farms, notably in parts of south-east Asia and elsewhere and are shipped to customers overseas by air.

One of the hardest problems faced by the early pioneers of tropical fish keeping was how to keep the water at a suitable temperature for the fish. Tanks were often stood on bases of slate, with a flame beneath, but this was far from satisfactory. The situation has since changed dramatically, and it is now easy to set up an aquarium for tropical fish without any difficulty. Visit your local aquarist or pet store, where a choice of both equipment and fish will be available. The growth of interest in fish-keeping generally is also mirrored in the rise of garden-centres; many now incorporate an aquatics section, catering for both coldwater and tropical fish enthusiasts. The cost of setting up a tank is surprisingly low, considering the advanced technology represented in a tropical aquarium. Many dealers will even offer a complete starter package, including fish, at a discount price. The subsequent maintenance costs are very low, while operational expenses will prove minimal.

A tropical aquarium offers a totally relaxing and attractive insight into the natural world. Unlike other pets, fish can be kept in apartments without any fear of causing offence to neighbours. In addition, they do not prove such a tie at holiday times as other animals, and can even be left for periods with slow release food blocks or automatic feeders without fear of polluting the water.

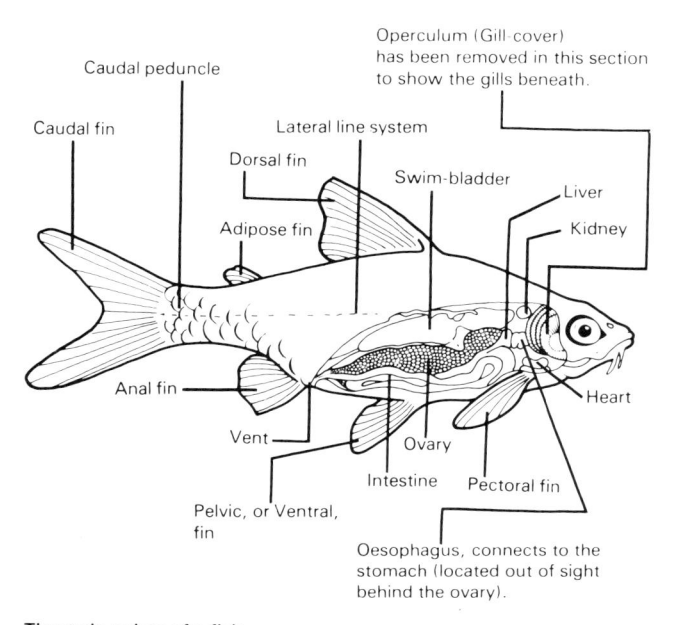

The main points of a fish, showing the internal anatomy:

Fish and their Characteristics

There is considerable diversity in the shape and size of fish available and such characteristics are usually a reflection of their natural environment. The popular Angelfish for example have evolved a tall, broad body shape, enabling them to swim around easily in the densely planted waters which they inhabit in the wild. Other fish, such as Hatchetfish, have adapted to live near the water's surface, catching unwary insects and darting away at the approach of danger. As would be expected, they have very good vision, and a mouth protruding in an upward direction, as well as a relatively straight back.

By way of contrast, certain fish forage for food on the river bed, where visibility may be poor. They have thus evolved additional sensory means of locating particles of food. The barbels of Catfish perform this function, being located close to the mouth, which protrudes downwards, facilitating ingestion of food. Fish, such as Tetras, occurring in the main area of water are forced to rely on a relatively compact body shape, and protection within a shoal, to escape potential predators, whereas the more sluggish Catfish are well-camouflaged to avoid detection. Some bottom-dwelling fish, such as the eel-like Loaches, may even burrow into the substrata, enabling them to remain largely hidden from view.

One of the pleasures of keeping tropical fish, especially with just one aquarium available, is setting up a community tank, with an assortment of fish in. The above points then assume practical significance, since the choice of fish should ideally be based on the selection of species that will occupy all depths of water, from the top to the bottom of the tank. There is also less risk of conflict if fish with different habits are included. Nevertheless, it must be remembered that some fish are predatory, even towards their own kind, and thus need to be kept individually, or with fish of the same size.

Anatomical Features

The majority of fish have a covering of scales, which protects them against infections, and aids their mobility. Propulsion is provided essentially by the fins. Although there is some variation, there are usually seven, of which the caudal or tail fin is the most significant for swimming purposes. Buoyancy is provided by the swim-bladder, which is filled with air. Disorders of this organ will often cause the fish to float at an abnormal angle in the water. Apart from their eyes, fish also have a unique means of detecting movement in their vicinity. This is provided by the so-called lateral line, that runs down both sides of the fish's body. It is filled with fluid that vibrates in response to pressure changes in the water, alerting the fish to the possible presence of danger nearby. The importance of the lateral line organs is greatest in the case of fish living under conditions where there is little light available. Indeed, the Blind Cave Fish relies on this system, along with an acute sense of smell, for its survival. As its name suggests, it is totally blind.

Fish extract oxygen from water as it flows over their gills, which are largely hidden beneath a flap known as the operculum present on both sides of the head, extending behind and below the eyes. Yet in some areas, there may be insufficient oxygen present in the water to sustain the fish. As a result, certain species have evolved auxiliary means of obtaining oxygen to ensure their survival. The so-called labyrinth fish are capable of breathing atmospheric air directly. This is achieved by means of the labyrinth organs, present within the gill cavities. The oxygen is absorbed directly into the bloodstream via the large surface area of fine tissue which comprises these organs. Indeed, one labyrinth fish known as the Climbing Perch is actually capable of living out of water for periods, typically during damp weather, relying directly on atmospheric oxygen at this time. It may wriggle overland from one area of water to another by this means. Some Catfish can also utilise air taken in at the water's surface, but by a different mechanism, and they too may occasionally venture onto land as a result. The oxygen in this instance is removed by an accessory respiratory organ present in the hind-gut, with the air actually being swallowed and voided via the anus.

Catfish are also unusual in that their bodies may not be covered in scales, but by bony scutes, which overlap, and these are popularly known as the Armoured Catfish. Other members of this large group of fish have neither scutes nor scales, but may be protected by their ability to produce electric shocks. They are often most active under conditions of semi-darkness, and this is another feature that must be considered in the aquarium environment.

1 Choosing Your Fish

One of the easiest groups of tropical fish, both to keep and breed successfully, are the livebearers, so-called because females actually produce live young, rather than eggs. There is no placental attachment however, as occurs in mammals. The eggs are simply retained within the female's body, where they develop until the young fish, known as fry, are ready to emerge. They are produced still curled up, but straighten once they come into contact with the water. Partly because of the free-breeding habits of these fish, mutations are commonly encountered in this group, and, in many instances, have been successfully developed by breeders to give a wide selection of fancy varieties.

Guppy

The greatest number of mutant forms have probably been produced in the case of the Guppy. This particular fish was one of the first tropical species to be kept successfully in aquarium surroundings, at the start of the present century. The Guppy is naturally found in parts of northern South America, including the islands of Trinidad and Barbados in the Caribbean, and its common name commemorates its discoverer, who was called Robert Guppy.

The requirements of guppies are relatively undemanding, and they can even tolerate temperatures as low as 15°C/64°F, but the optimum is about 26°C/79°F. They are easily sexed, with females being considerably larger than their male counterparts, attaining a maximum size of about 6 cm (2½ ins) when fully grown, and proving duller in overall coloration.

Wild guppies show considerable variation in their markings, but selective breeding of mutations has given rise to changes not only in colour, but also in the shape of the fins. Such mutants are known under various names. One of the most spectacular is probably the Veiltail form where the caudal fin has become greatly enlarged. In the case of the Fantail, the dorsal fin is also considerably bigger than normal. There are numerous other modifications of this type, yet guppies with more elaborate fins can be at risk from fin-nipping in a community aquarium and generally prove more delicate. It is possible to improve the coloration of these fish by means of a suitable colour food, which will emphasise red coloration in particular. Special diets are available for this purpose, but in any event, guppies are undemanding in their feeding habits. They will take dried food, along with vegetable matter, browsing on plants in their aquarium, and also accept livefood if this is offered. In terms of water chemistry, guppies do best under conditions where the water is slightly hard, and the pH is on the alkaline side of neutral.

The number of fry produced by a female guppy is related in part to the female's length, with bigger individuals producing a relatively large brood, compared with their smaller counterparts. Following mating, it will take a variable time for the fry to develop in the female's body. When guppies are kept in water maintained at 25°C/77°F, this process takes about four weeks, whereas at a higher temperature around 32°C/92°F it can fall to just 19 days, although the lifespan of the fish themselves also appears to be reduced. A brood may be comprised of up to 100 fry, and these should be reared in separate quarters if possible, since adults will prove cannibalistic towards their offspring.

Mollies

These members of the live-bearing tooth carp group are naturally found in brackish water, in the vicinity of the Gulf of Mexico. Nine species are recognised, but only about half are commonly kept in aquaria. They do best in water to which sea salt has been added, at the level of about a teaspoonful per 10 litres (2½ gal). A characteristic sign of ill-health in Mollies is the condition known as shimmying. Affected fish remain stationary, shaking with clasped fins. Observe fish prior to purchase for any signs of this complaint. It may be possible to overcome the symptoms by increasing the temperature of the water but it is likely that the fish may be suffering from an infection if they have been kept in freshwater with no added salt.

Mollies are essentially herbivorous in their feeding habits, and are capable of damaging plants in their aquarium, so that vegetation chosen should be relatively tough and able to withstand their attentions. Encouraging algal growth by keeping the tank well-lit will provide a natural source of food for these fish, which can be supplemented with proprietary items. Fresh greenfood, such as cress or lettuce cut into very small pieces, can also be offered to mollies.

Breeding follows the typical pattern for this group of fish. The male's anal fin is adapted to form a copulatory organ, known as the gonopodium, which channels the semen into the female's vent. Courtship in fact can be a prolonged process, and subsequently, the gravid female can be recognised by the presence of a black spot, typically evident on both sides of the body. Mollies are especially delicate at this stage and will abort readily, so they must be left undisturbed if possible. One mating will suffice to fertilise several successive clutches of eggs.

Female mollies are again larger than their male counterparts, and are generally duller in terms of overall appearance. In the case of the Sailfin Molly, the dorsal fin of the adult male is also considerably larger than that of the female, although this distinction is not apparent in young fish. It is preferable to keep males apart, as they tend to fight. Females may produce up to 80 fry, after a period of two months or so. The young fish develop relatively slowly, and may not breed themselves until they are over a year old. They can live for at least three years, and once mature, females may breed almost continuously, producing broods in rapid succession under favourable conditions. A very similar species is the Mexican or Giant Sailfin Molly, which grows slightly larger, with females attaining a maximum size of about 17.5 cm (7 ins). The dorsal fin of these fish is broader, and is positioned closer to the head than in the case of the Sailfin Molly. The patterning present on the dorsal fin also tends to be circular instead of elongated in shape. There is some variation in colour, and occasionally black individuals are seen.

The role of Sailfin Mollies in the development of the popular Black Molly is unclear, although certainly these fish are of hybrid ancestry. Males have a large, slightly curved dorsal fin and are consistently black in colour, whereas females tend to show more variable coloration, with only traces of black apparent in some instances. Indeed, a number of further hybrids are now recognised, some of which show variations in the shape of both dorsal and caudal fins. Many of these forms are believed to be descended from the Pointed-mouth Molly, which is similar to the Sailfin Molly, but has a smaller dorsal fin, reflected in its alternative name of Short-finned Molly. These fish tend to frequent the upper area of the tank, and like other members of the family Poecilidae, are suitable occupants for the community aquarium. The water should be slightly alkaline and a temperature in the range 23-28°C/73-78°F will suit them well.

Unfortunately, mollies tend to eat their fry, and for breeding purposes, females can be transferred easily to a separate tank, and then be removed after the brood has been produced. The fry themselves are not difficult to rear on brine shrimp nauplii and fry foods. Alternatively, if the tank is densely-planted, the fry may be able to escape their rapacious elders, so there will be no need to catch the

Golden Angelfish

Pearl Gourami

gravid female, and risk causing the loss of her developing brood.

Platies

The description of 'Platy' is an abbreviated form of the old generic name for these fish, which was *Platypoecilus*. They occur in Central America, notably in Mexico, and show the typical characteristics of the family, with males being both smaller and brighter in colour than females. Two forms are normally recognised, being the Platy itself and the Variegated Platy, but widespread hybridisation has occurred so that obtaining pure stock may not be easy. The dorsal fin can provide a means of distinguishing between the two species, since it is generally larger and broader in the case of the Variegated Platy.

A number of attractive colour forms have been developed. The Red Platy, as its name suggests, is red overall and there is also a similar yellow variety. In the case of the Red and Yellow Wagtails, the colour of the caudal fin is black, while the rest of the body coloration remains unaltered. The Tuxedo Platies actually have split markings, with red or green upperparts, while the bottom half of their bodies is black. By contrast, the wild forms of the Platy may appear rather dull.

Unlike the mollies, these fish do not require salt to be added to the water in their tank. In other respects, however, their management should be similar. Platies are mature from about six months onwards, and although early broods may be small, mature females can produce as many as a 150 fry at a time. Like

Platy

Red Oscar

other live-bearers, they will eat large quantities of insect larvae, and a supply of gnat larvae will rapidly stimulate breeding condition in these fish. Indeed, in certain areas in the wild, live-bearers are greatly valued as a means of controlling mosquitos and thus malaria, by eating the aquatic larval stage in the mosquito's life-cycle.

Swordtails

The Swordtail is similar in appearance to the platies, although males possess the swordlike elongation of the lower rays of the caudal fin which has given rise to their popular name. Indeed, if kept in the company of platies, then hybridisation between these fish may occur. Their requirements are identical, and they do best in a planted tank, with a central clear area available for swimming. Females lack the characteristic sword, and are slightly larger, attaining a maximum size approaching 12.5 cm (5 ins) overall.

Selective breeding has led to the emergence of many varieties of Swordtail, which in some cases parallel those recognised in platies, such as the Red and Wagtail Swordtails. A black form as well as an albino have also been bred. Fin changes are apparent in some individuals, giving rise to lyre-tailed as well as hi-fin swordtails, where the dorsal fin itself is enlarged. With the wide selection available, it is best to select a particular variety, and concentrate on breeding fish of this type or colour, rather than having a mixed group. Swordtails naturally occur in shoals, although they can also be kept in smaller numbers in a community tank. Some individuals can prove rather aggressive, but these fish are usually peaceful, and easy to cater for. Occasionally, swordtails undergo a spontaneous sex-change, with a female developing a sword. This need not be a cause for concern. Expect large broods from bigger females: well over 200 fry have been recorded from just a single brood, although in most cases up to half this number can be anticipated, depending upon the size of the female.

Half-Beak

A member of the family which includes the flying fishes, the Half-beak, like the mollies, will benefit from the addition of sea salt to the aquarium water. These long and relatively narrow fish are characterised by the beak-like protrusion of their lower jaw. They tend to be nervous, especially when transferred to new accommodation, and may injure themselves unless adequate cover is available. Males are easily distinguished by a red mark on their dorsal fin. This species has a wide distribution over much of South-east Asia, and coloration can very accordingly. Half-beaks feed on a variety of foodstuffs, often lurking just below the water's surface to grab insects.

Although unrelated to the live-bearing toothcarps, the Half-beak female nevertheless produces live young. The fry take about two months to develop in her body, and the characteristic elongation of the lower jaw will not start to become apparent for another five weeks or so. The young fish are about 1 cm (⅓ in) overall at first, and will grow to a maximum size of 7 cm (2¾ ins), with females proving relatively small; up to 20 fry can be anticipated at a time. As they mature, the young fish will need to be separated, since males are likely to start fighting each other. While not as easy to breed successfully as the preceding species, the Half-beak makes an unusual and interesting aquarium subject, requiring similar water conditions, with the addition of some floating plants at the surface, beneath which the fish will spend much of their time.

Egg-Laying Tooth-Carps

This group of fish reproduce by means of eggs. In some cases, these are laid in amongst vegetation, whereas in other species, spawning takes place directly on to the substrate of the pool.

Some egg-laying tooth-carps, also known as killifish, need fairly specialist conditions, but others can be kept satisfactorily in a community tank. These include members of the genera *Pachypanchax*, *Rivulus* and *Epiplatys*, although generally, it will be preferable to set up an aquarium to cater specifically for each group of these fish. This is because in the wild, they normally inhabit water that is derived directly from rain, living in pools heavily contaminated with organic matter, so that they are used to soft and acid water conditions.

Playfair's Panchax occurs in East Africa, extending to the Seychelles, and attains a maximum size of 10 cm (4 ins). Females are duller overall, being predominantly brown with an area of black close to their dorsal fin. The swollen appearance of these fish, which can be confused with the symptoms of dropsy, stems from the unusual arrangement of their scales and is especially noticeable during the breeding period. Eggs are laid in vegetation, or alternatively, in the aquarium, on an artificial nylon spawning mop. Most killifish feed close to the surface, preferring livefoods, but this particular species will adapt more readily than most to a diet of dried food. Some individuals prove aggressive however, and should be watched accordingly.

The Green Rivulus is a South American killifish, which can grow to about 8 cm (3¼ ins) and has a relatively elongated body. Females again are less colourful, being predominantly brown in coloration. Spawning is relatively straightforward, with the eggs being deposited on vegetation. These killifish frequent upper reaches of water, and may even leave water occasionally, resting on floating vegetation. As with all killifish, a suitable cover over their aquarium is essential, as they are capable of leaping out of the water. Livefood, such as fruit flies, will be appreciated by these fish, in addition to dried foods.

Killifish have a wide distribution, being represented on all continents apart from Australia. They occur throughout Africa, apart from the southernmost tip and many popular aquarium species originate here. A number of *Epiplatys* species for example occur in West Africa, of which the most colourful is the Rocket Panchax. Females lack the red and blue coloration present on the fins of males. They do not differ significantly in their requirements from the preceding species, favouring a water temperature around 26°C/79°F, although they can prove reluctant to take proprietary foods, showing a strong preference for livefood. The eggs of the Rocket Panchax should hatch within about three weeks. It is preferable to remove the spawning mops with the eggs attached to separate accommodation as soon as spawning has taken place. *Epiplatys* species generally are not aggressive.

Although in the wild, most substrate-spawning killifish will only live for a year, until their pools dry up, they can live much longer under aquarium conditions. They rank amongst the most colourful members of the family, and do best when kept in groups, with several females to each male. The substrate of their aquarium should be a layer of peat, at least 2.5 cm (1 in) deep. Here the killifish females will burrow to lay their eggs individually. From the outset, it will take several days to establish a tank, since at first the peat will float on the surface, until it is saturated. Only plants that will float should be included in tanks for these killifish. No other decor is provided, and lighting should not be excessively bright. The eggs will need special treatment, as described later.

The Lyretail Killifish actually vary in their breeding habits. The Lyretail itself, occurring in West Africa, commonly deposits its eggs on plants, but may also spawn in the substrate. Females, as in other killifish, are duller in coloration and, in this instance, have rounded tails. Unfortunately, some of the most striking members of this group also prove aggressive. The Steel-blue Lyretail from Nigeria fits in this category. Two colour forms are recognised, with males either being mainly yellow, or bright blue with red markings. A larger spe-

Harlequin

Half Banded Barbs

cies, attaining a maximum size of about 12 cm (4¾ ins) is the Blue Gularis. In this instance, females are also quite colourful, being green and red. The caudal fin of males of this species forms three distinct lobes.

Amongst the East African species of killifish, the *Nothobranchius* rank amongst the most popular, although they do tend to be short-lived. Eggs are again laid in the substrate. As a result, it is possible to purchase eggs rather than adult fish, and hatch them in the aquarium, which gives a fascinating insight into the life-cycle of these fish.

Annual killifish also occur in South America, although African species tend to predominate in aquaria. Their requirements are similar however, with the fish usually being kept in small single species groups, comprised of one male alongside several females. Livefood will encourage breeding activity, with spawning itself taking place at intervals over the course of a week or longer. Amongst the South American species available are the Featherfin Panchax and the Dwarf Argentine Pearl Fish.

Barbs and Related Species

The members of the family *Cyprinidae* have a wide distribution through the Old World, although they are absent from South America and Australia. This is a large family, comprised of nearly 1500 species, which typically inhabit slow-flowing water, often living in shoals. The coldwater Goldfish is well-known, while a number of other species are equally popular amongst tropical fish enthusiasts.

Indeed, barbs are attractive shoaling fish

Barbs

Rosy Barbs

that prove generally easy to maintain in the tropical aquarium. Although they can be kept in slightly hard water, breeding is more likely to occur when these fish are kept under soft water conditions. A water temperature in the range 23-26°C/73°-79°F suits them well, and suitable aeration should be provided, as these species are found in moving water. They will eat a variety of foods readily, including proprietary brands of dry food, with livefood proving a valuable conditioner for breeding purposes.

One of the easiest and most attractive barbs for the aquarium is the Rosy, which naturally occurs in northern India and can grow to 14 cm (5½ ins). Unlike some members of the group, they lack barbels, with females being paler than their male counterparts. Spawning follows a period of intense activity, with the male pursuing the female vigorously. It may be preferable to transfer them to a separate tank beforehand, where the fish will not be able to eat their eggs. The fry should hatch within a day or so, and are not difficult to rear on standard fry foods.

The Rosy Barb is one of the medium-sized species in this genus, whereas the striking Tinfoil Barb can grow as large as 35 cm (14 ins). This particular barb needs to be kept in a suitably sized aquarium in groups on its own, rather than in the company of its smaller relatives. These barbs jump quite readily, and will damage plants, although the provision of vegetable matter as part of their diet will help to deter such predations.

By way of contrast, the small Golden Dwarf Barb will not exceed 4 cm (1½ in), even when adult. In spite of their size however, these are not delicate fish and are more tolerant of low water temperatures than related species. Indeed, they are most at home in water heated to only 20-22°C/68-72°F. Females are broader overall than males, with both sexes having semi-transparent bodies. They spawn quite readily, especially when livefood is included in their diet, and will often leave their eggs unmolested, although it is preferable to have a separate spawning tank if possible, with plants included, especially if the barbs normally form part of a mixed community. Their fry develop rapidly, and should emerge about a day after spawning has taken place.

Another small species, with similar requirements, although requiring a higher water temperature in the range of 22-25°C/72-77°F is the Island or Chequer Barb which originates from the island of Sumatra, off the coast of South-east Asia. They are easy to sex — males have red dorsal fins with black edges, whereas those of females are basically yellow. These particular barbs make lively aquarium occupants, and show to best effect in shoals, although males may sometimes disagree with each other. Their alternative name of Chequer Barb is derived from the dark markings present on the sides of their bodies.

Another species sometimes described as the Sumatra Barb is usually better known as the Tiger Barb, and has a definitive striped patterning on its body. Males are brighter in coloration than females, with red tips to their fins. Inhabiting fast-flowing, clear water, these fish must not be overcrowded, and need to be kept in well-oxygenated surroundings. The related Five-banded Barb can be distinguished by an incomplete bar running down from the dorsal fin on either side of the body. Unfortunately this group of barbs will frequently persecute other fish by nipping at their fins, especially those with elaborate fins, such as Angelfish. This vice is more often displayed by solitary individuals however, rather than when a shoal of these barbs is being kept together. They are prolific fish overall, with females producing as many as 1000 eggs at a single spawning. A male will drive a female hard prior to egg-laying, and ultimately the eggs will be deposited in amongst plants, where they should hatch within a day or so.

Two attractive species of barb which are well-worth considering for a community tank originate from Sri Lanka. The Purple-headed or Black Ruby grows to about 6 cm (2½ ins), with females being paler than males and lacking the dark edges to their fins. It is easy to detect the onset of breeding condition in this case, since not only do females swell with eggs, but their mates become much more colourful, with their red heads assuming a purplish hue, and green coloration becomes noticeably brighter along their backs. Although active, these are not aggressive fish, and keeping several males in the company of fewer females tends to ensure that some are in breeding condition throughout most of the year. An increase in water temperature tends to encourage spawning, while the water itself must be soft. Floating plants should be included in the aquarium for these barbs, along with plants that are suitably robust, since they may be attacked by the fish. Indeed, like other barbs, the Black Ruby is omnivorous in its feeding habits.

The Cherry Barb is even smaller than these Sri Lankan species, not growing much beyond 4.5 cm (1¾ ins). These fish can be identified by the presence of a pair of small barbels at the corner of their upper jaw. Males are especially attractive, with their bright red coloration becoming particularly striking during the breeding period. Their fins are also reddish, whereas those of females are paler. Like the preceding species, the Cherry Barb inhabits fairly shaded stretches of water, so that their aquarium should not be brightly lit. Floating plants on the water's surface will help to create a secluded environment for the fish. Again, soft water is essential for spawning, although these particular barbs are not as prolific as some members of the group. In the first instance, relatively fewer eggs are produced at a single spawning, and the fry are very small, making rearing in the early stages more difficult. Unfortunately, the Cherry Barb tends to be shy by nature, but will not molest other fish in a community tank.

Other members of the family Cyprinidae frequently seen in aquaria are the Danios. These are small fish; indeed, the so-called Giant Danio only grows to a maximum size of less than 15 cm (6 ins). They are attractive fish that show to best effect when kept in a shoal. Danios are not aggressive, even towards each other. They are capable of jumping however, and their tank will need to be covered. The bluish-green stripes on the sides of these fish provide the means of distinguishing between the sexes. These curl vertically in females at the base of the caudal fin. In order to encourage spawning, livefood should be provided. As many as 1000 eggs may be laid, with females spawning about every month if kept under favourable conditions. They should be transferred from their breeding accommodation as soon as the eggs are laid, because otherwise these may eaten. This species occurs in Sri Lanka, and western parts of India.

Another Danio found in the same area is the Bengal Danio. It is silver overall, with greenish-blue flanks. As with the Giant Danio, introduce the female to the spawning tank first, and ensure that fine-leaved plants like *Myriophyllum* are included. These will ultimately attract the female when she is due to spawn, and help to protect the newly-laid eggs from being consumed almost immediately.

Zebra Danios are justifiably popular. They are small fish, growing to about 5 cm (2 ins) overall, with females being generally larger than males. The markings and coloration on their flanks have given rise to their common name, with longitudinal pale stripes on a greyish-blue background running from head to tail. Zebra Danios prove very undemanding fish, and are thus quite suitable for the newcomer to tropical fish-keeping. A breeding tank should be set up as recommended previously for other Danios. They can similarly be kept together in shoals, preferring the upper layer of water.

Another South-east Asian species often available is the beautiful Pearl Danio with its iridescent body showing to best effect under conditions of relatively bright light. Limited exposure to sunlight entering the room will

Blue Gourami

Kissing Gouramis

not harm these fish, and may well encourage a female to spawn. This normally takes place in the morning, with perhaps five hundred eggs being laid over a period of hours. Adequate protection must be available if the spawn is not to be eaten by the adult fish.

The genus *Rasbora* contains about 30 species, which are found throughout South-east Asia. Although these are relatively straighforward to maintain under aquarium conditions, breeding these fish can prove more problematical than in the case of Danios or Barbs. Successes are becoming more common however, and it seems that, at least with some species, the provision of soft, acid water, in a darkened spawning tank planted with *Cryptocorynes* or similar broad-leaved plants is most likely to lead to success. Keeping the fish in small groups for spawning purposes can also prove beneficial. It can be difficult to sex certain species of rasbora, so that it is preferable to keep them in groups in any event. Under such conditions, it has proved possible to breed Harlequin Fish. These are relatively small fish, growing to a maximum size of about 4.5 cm (1¾ ins).

A larger species of rasbora is the Scissortail so-called because of its tail movements, which resemble the movements of scissors. A peat base to the aquarium, as suggested previously for certain killifish, is to be recommended in this instance. This will also suit the Spotted Rasbora. The smallest member of the group, growing to about 2.5 cm (1 in) overall, the Spotted Rasbora needs similar water conditions to those described previously. These fish are best in groups on their own. Partial water

Golden Gourami

Angelfish

changes are to be recommended to retain water purity, with some aquarists using rainwater to refill the tank, in the hope of encouraging breeding activity. Rasboras will feed on a variety of foodstuffs, often showing a preference for livefood. If a pair do spawn, it may be the fry and not the eggs themselves that are at risk from the adult fish. It takes about a day for the eggs to hatch, and the fry will remain largely hidden in the vegetation at first for two or three days.

There are various other members of the family Cyprinidae which are popular aquarium occupants. The Red-tailed Black Shark, in spite of its fearsome name, belongs to this group of fish, and is in no way related to the sharks. They are easy fish to maintain, but may fight amongst themselves. Adequate cover must be included in their aquarium, and supplementary herbivorous material should be provided, in addition to a standard diet. Occurring in Thailand, the Red-tailed Black Shark rarely grows beyond 12.5 cm (5 ins) under aquarium conditions, although bigger fish have been reported from the wild. Breedings under aquarium conditions are unusual at present.

Another fish which will browse contentedly on algae in a community tank is the Flying Fox. These fish also tend to spend much of their time near the floor of the aquarium, and with territorial natures, outbreaks of fighting may occur if a number of Flying Foxes are housed together. It appears that this species has yet to be bred in the confines of an aquarium; in any event, the Flying Fox is not actually a difficult fish to keep, and proves quite amenable to other fish in a community tank. Soft water, heated in the range of 22-27°C/72-81°F, will suit them well. Adequate retreats must be incorporated into the floor of the aquarium for them.

Characins

The characins as a group are confined to Africa, and parts of Central and South America where the largest concentration of species is found. There are various families within the sub-order, of which the family Characidae is probably of greatest significance for aquarists, since it includes the popular and often highly colourful tetras, such as the Neon Tetra which is found in the upper Amazon. These fish look especially striking when kept in shoals. The water in their aquarium needs to be soft, and on the acid side of neutral in pH terms while the tank itself should be relatively dark and well-planted. Neon Tetras had a reputation for being delicate, partly because of their susceptibility to parasites, but with vast numbers now being bred in captivity, this image is being lost. They are omnivorous in their feeding habits, but rather than seeking food at the water's surface, these fish prefer to feed in the lower stretches of water.

When spawning, Neon Tetras must have a tank with a dark substrate, such as peat, and a low level of illumination. This is because their eggs are liable to be destroyed by light. Assuming the fish are in good condition, they should produce eggs within a week of being transferred to the spawning tank. The young fry hatch in about a day, and will rest close to the surface in a darkened tank, effectively supported by surface tension. If disturbed, they will drop to the bottom. Some breeders actually cover the sides of the spawning tank with black plastic to exclude as much light as possible in order to encourage breeding and assist in the rearing of the fry.

Another brightly-coloured tetra which has similar requirements is the Cardinal. Again, it is difficult to sex these fish visually, but since they do best in shoals, there is likely to be at least one pair within the group. As a guide, most female characins can be recognised by their rounded body shape, especially when in breeding condition, and their dorsal fins may be less prominent than in males. This can also apply to the anal fins as well.

The Blind Cave Fish from Mexico is an extreme example of a species that lives in dark surroundings. It inhabits subterranean waters and apart from loss of eyesight, this fish lacks colour pigment, being whitish in coloration, with its blood giving the body a pinkish tone overall. An attractive aquarium featuring plenty of rockwork and similar retreats can be set up without difficulty for these fish, keeping lighting at a low intensity. Breeding behaviour is typical of the characin group, with the fry becoming free-swimming about four days after hatching. Interestingly, they are not blind at first, but skin grows over their eyes, leaving them to rely on their other senses for survival as they mature.

Another oddity in terms of its appearance is the Disc Tetra which has a flattened and broad body shape, unlike that of other tetras. It can grow to nearly 12.5 cm (5 ins), but its care should be similar to that for other tetras, and these fish will do best in shoals, housed in suitably spacious accommodation.

One characin with a similar body shape to the Disc Tetra but a savage reputation is the Piranha. These are not social fish, and may even eat members of their own species. Never house two individuals of different sizes together for this reason. They have powerful teeth and feed readily on a variety of animal matter, including worms and insects. Although the popularity of piranhas rose sharply several years ago, they prove rather dull fish for the aquarium, and certainly cannot be included in a community tank. Conditions as recommended for tetras will suit them well, although they are now classified in a separate family.

Tetras generally are relatively small fish, usually not exceeding 7.5 cm (3 ins) in length, and some species only grow to about half this size. While the South American tetras are very popular as shoaling fish for the community aquarium, African species are also available on occasions. These include the Congo Tetra, which is relatively easy to sex, since males have more elaborate fins, and grow bigger than their female counterparts. Their care should be identical to the New World species. Soft water with a pH reading that is just acid will suit them well.

The term 'tetra' is often applied to all small members of the family, but not in every instance. The X-ray Fish, so-called because of its semi-transparent body, is another characin from South America, and grows to about 5 cm (2 ins) overall. Although not difficult to keep, in the standard conditions for tetras, X-ray Fish are not easy to breed. Compatibility may be a factor in some breeding disappointments, and a choice of partner can have a beneficial effect.

Catfish

There are about 2000 recognised species of catfish, which are concentrated notably in South America and Africa. Many can grow to a large size, making them unsuitable for the average home aquarium. Some members of the group are very popular however, and add interest to the floor of the aquarium where they will forage for food. Catfish tend to frequent muddy water where visibility is poor, and as such, will not thrive under conditions of bright light. Indeed, some are almost nocturnal in their habits.

One of the most unusual catfish is undoubtedly the Glass Catfish. Apart from the lack of scales, which is a feature of this group of fish, the body is entirely transparent, apart from the head where there are two long barbels protruding from the upper jaw. Unfortunately, Glass Catfish do tend to be delicate, and will spend much of their time hiding amongst vegetation in the aquarium. They do best when kept in groups, but they can be difficult to wean onto dried foods, and if permitted so to do, will feed almost exclusively on daphnia. Perhaps as a result of their unusual anatomy, they seem very susceptible to the parasitic disease called white-spot, which reveals itself by the presence of tiny white dots over the body of the fish. It is a contagious disease, as explained later.

Members of the genus *Corydoras*, like the

Glass Catfish, are also diurnal, and this has contributed towards their popularity in the aquarium. In addition, they do not grow large, and can be bred successfully. In this instance, a surplus of male fish is likely to prove advantageous. These should be introduced to a female in a spawning tank, with all the fish being removed as soon as egg laying has finished. This can take place over several hours and the fish will readily consume their own spawn if permitted to do so. Eggs are produced in small batches, being laid on plants, and, at a temperature of 26°C/79°F, should hatch in a week.

Loaches

Like the catfish, loaches tend to frequent the floor of the aquarium and may hide amongst rockwork and other decor, especially during the day. Probably the most striking species suitable for the community tank is the Clown Loach, which will live happily alongside catfish. Soft water and a temperature around 26°C/79°F will suit them well. They are slow-growing fish, and do not appear to have been bred to date under aquarium conditions. Clown loaches will take a variety of foodstuffs however, and in the company of catfish, make useful scavengers on the aquarium floor. Some loaches can prove aggressive though, and for this reason, the Banded or Tiger Loach should be kept on its own if possible, and must not be overcrowded, as this will lead to fighting.

Cichlids

The cichlids are a fairly stocky group of fish which tend to be unsuitable for the mixed aquarium, since they can be both aggressive and destructive, as well as growing to a large size, in certain instances. Some, notably those from lakes in the African Rift Valley, need hard water, with an alkaline pH whereas the South American Discus will require water that is both soft and acid. These particular fish have been bred in a range of colours, but are certainly not the easiest cichlids to maintain and breed successfully.

Undoubtedly the most popular members of this family in aquarist circles are the Angelfish which can be recognised immediately by their tall, flat, striped bodies. While small Angelfish are frequently recommended for the community tank, they are not entirely suitable in this regard. Their shape dictates that ultimately they will need a deep tank, as they can grow to as much as 25 cm (10 ins) in total height. The fins of Angelfish are also liable to be damaged by other fish in a mixed tank, so that overall, these elegant fish are best accommodated in a shoal on their own. The breeding habits of cichlids generally are interesting, and the Angelfish is no exception, fastidiously cleaning a chosen site, such as rockwork, before laying takes place. Then after the fry have hatched they are guarded in a pit by the adult fish for a week or so. Various colour forms are now quite common, including an attractive golden-yellow variety as well as a veil-tailed form.

The water for Angelfish needs to be soft, and bordering on the acid side of the pH scale. Feeding presents no special problems, although they will eat smaller fish, and may occasionally consume their own fry. Cichlid

Malawi Cichlid

Large Cichlid

diets are available and can be used with other items such as livefood if desired.

Another South American cichlid of striking appearance is the Oscar or Velvet Chichlid, which can grow to nearly twice the length of an Angelfish, up to 30 cm (12 ins). The black 'eye spot' surrounded by an orange ring at the base of the caudal tailfin is a distinguishing feature of these large fish, which, in spite of their fearsome appearance, do become quite tame. They must have a large tank however, and an adequate filtration system. There is little point in including plants as these will soon be dug up and destroyed. Oscars can produce a large number of fry at a single spawning, and these will again be guarded by their parents. It may be necessary to deter them from either spawning on or damaging the heater in their aquarium. In either case, this should be wrapped in plastic netting of the appropriate mesh dimensions, which will still allow free circulation of water, while preventing the fish reaching the outer casing of the heater. Oscars have healthy appetites, and must therefore not be mixed with other, smaller fish.

2 Housing

The introduction of silicone rubber sealant to aquarium manufacturing led to a rapid demise in the traditional heavy tank with an iron framework and puttied glass. It has also meant that aquaria of literally any shape can be constructed, and triangular designs are now quite common. Yet these are not entirely satisfactory in many cases because of their dimensions. It is best to purchase a relatively large aquarium at the outset since not only will this give the fish a reasonable area for swimming, it will also allow them space to grow, without the need to change the tank later. Yet while the bonding power of silicone rubber sealant is both versatile and strong, an aquarium full of water exerts considerable pressure on the glass, which will suffer from any unevenness in the surface on which it is stood. It is for this reason that aquaria made using silicone rubber sealant are normally stood on a polystyrene base, which will be virtually invisible once the aquarium is set up.

Moulded plastic tanks are also available, and are lighter to carry than their glass counterparts. The major drawback of plastic however is that its visual appeal deteriorates much more quickly than in the case of glass. Scratches become readily apparent, and discoloration may follow, with algae actually colonising the damaged areas. For clarity of viewing over a period of time therefore, a glass aquarium is preferable, but plastic tanks are useful for quarantining, and spawning purposes.

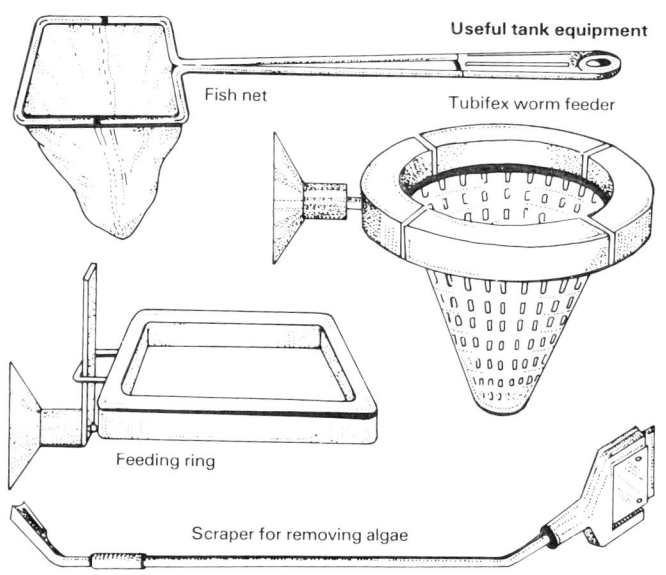

Useful tank equipment

Fish net

Tubifex worm feeder

Feeding ring

Scraper for removing algae

Equipment and Decor

There have been considerable advances in the technology involved in aquarium equipment, with micro-chips now ensuring very accurate control of water temperature. Although it is possible to purchase heaters and thermostats as individual units, the combined 'heater-stat' is preferable in most cases. The heating component is available in various wattages, typically ranging from 50 to 300W. As a guide, allow 10W for every 4·5 litres (1 gal) of water. Individual heaters are more suited for larger tanks, where two may be operating off a single thermostat, although heater-stats can be used as an alternative.

A visual guide to the water temperature is provided by a thermometer. There are various types available, some of which fit inside the tank, but the digital thermometer is now favoured by many aquarists, being easy to read and inconspicuous. This type of thermometer comes in the form of a thin strip which sticks to the front of the aquarium. It is important to remember that the figure shown can be distorted by being touched; children seem attracted to the visual display, and can inadvertently alter the temperature. In addition, some digital thermometers cannot be moved with safety once they have been stuck in position.

A light above the tank serves to highlight the aquarium, and will benefit the tank occupants, especially if one of the so-called 'natural' fluorescent tubes is used. These mimic the wavelengths present in sunlight, and thus encourage plant growth as well as emphasising the colours of the fish themselves. Fluorescent tubes in any event are preferable to tungsten light bulbs, because they will not affect the temperature of the water, whereas domestic bulbs can emit considerable amounts of heat, which build up in the confined space of the aquarium.

Several basic types of filter can be obtained, all of which serve to keep the water free from organic impurities. Under normal circumstances, waste produced by the fish will be broken down from toxic ammonia to nitrite, and then finally nitrate by bacteria. The nitrate is then utilised by plants for their growth, acting as a fertiliser. This forms the basis of the nitrogen cycle, and this principle is incorporated in the undergravel or U/G filter. As its name suggests, this fits directly on to the floor of the aquarium. A layer of gravel above forms the filter layer, where the population of aerobic bacteria become established. In order to work effectively, the system must not be overloaded, and sufficient oxygen needs to be available to sustain the bacterial population. An air pump is therefore included as part of this system and assists in circulating the water through the tank, including the filter bed. The vibrator type of air pump tends to be cheaper than the piston designs, and although it may be noisier, it tends to need less maintenance. It is important to position the pump above the water level in either case, so that no water can track down the tubing if the power supply is lost. Alternatively, a valve can be inserted in the air line to prevent this occurrence. Never cover the pump as this will cause overheating, but if the noise proves distracting, it may help to place it on a felt base.

The tubing from the air pump may connect to an air stone in the aquarium, releasing a stream of bubbles into the water. Although this appears to have the effect of oxygenating the water, its main function is to improve the actual circulation of water within the aquarium. It is possible to vary the size of the bubbles being passed out via the air stone, which can be in the form of tank ornaments, such as a diver. An air-lift performs a similar function. As a direct adjunct to an undergravel filter, the air-lift is formed by the clear plastic tube that fits vertically on to the filter plate. A concentrated stream of air bubbles is forced to the surface, moving water with them.

Air is also necessary for mechanical, as distinct from biological, filters. Water in this instance is passed through a series of filter media that draw debris out of the water. The units themselves can fit either inside or outside the tank. Although it may be more unsightly in this latter locality, the filter is much easier to service in this position, as will be necessary at regular intervals. Special filter wool, which removes solid debris, and activated charcoal positioned between two layers of filter wool are included in the box filter, with the charcoal serving to extract toxic substances present in solution. Other items sometimes included in a box filter are peat, and sand, but generally, it is preferable to opt only for the special materials sold in aquatic outlets. Indeed, likely alternatives may well prove injurious for the fish, as in the case of glass wool.

The floor of the aquarium is usually covered with gravel, and again, this can be purchased from an aquatic store. Especially for fish that prefer soft water, gravel that is guaranteed free from lime is to be recommended. Particle size is also significant, especially if an undergravel filter is to be used, since fine gravel will prevent passage of water, and hence debris, down through the filter bed. Coarse gravel conversely will take food down too quickly, and does not permit the development of an adequate population of bacteria. A particle size of about 3 mm is to be recommended as a compromise, allowing as a guide about 1 kg of gravel for 4·5 litres of water (2lb per gal). Although coloured gravel is available, this can look very artificial in the completed aquarium and the dye must be fast, otherwise the water will soon be clouded with a potentially toxic dye. In any event, the gravel needs to be washed thoroughly, preferably in a plastic colander under a running tap, so as to remove dirt before it is placed in the tank. Dirty gravel will otherwise lead to an unpleasant scum forming at the water's surface.

Some rockwork may be included in the aquarium, providing a retreat for the fish or a spawning site in some cases. It is vital though to choose only insoluble rocks, such as slate, granite and quartz. Any limestone for example will dissolve over a period of time, hardening the water. Check that rockwork is firmly positioned, and cannot be dislodged by the fish, as clearly this could smash the glass side of an aquarium with catastrophic results.

Submerged wood, in the form of tree branches or roots, is also frequently seen in aquaria, but today, artificial substitutes are available. This avoids the need to prepare wood over a period of weeks to make it suitable for the aquarium, and there is no risk of artificial wood either introducing disease, or simply rotting in the aquarium.

In order to complete the natural appearance of the aquarium, it is usual to include plants, although this is not practical in every instance, since some fish will destroy vegetation, either by digging in the gravel or eating the plants directly. Plants will utilise nitrate produced by bacteria from organic waste, and thus help to purify the water, as well as acting as spawning sites for many species. A wide variety of aquarium plants can be obtained, with specialist nurseries catering for this side of the hobby, although aquarist stores also usually have a wide selection available.

It is best to design an initial plan for the aquarium incorporating plants. As a guide, it is usual to position plants that grow quite large, such as *Sagittaria*, towards the rear of the aquarium, with smaller plants in the foreground, allowing an adequate clear area where the fish can swim freely and be clearly seen. A dealer will be able to advise on the choice of specific plants for a tank. Choose only plants that appear healthy, showing signs of vigorous growth, with no yellowing of their leaves. In most instances, truly aquatic plants absorb nutrients via their leaves, rather than roots which serve essentially to provide anchorage. Plants can be set directly into the aquarium gravel, although their roots may interfere with the holes of an undergravel filter.

Setting up the Tank

The siting of the tank is an important consideration, and the position chosen should be out of direct sunlight. Excessive illumination will favour algal growth, and more seriously, may cause the water temperature to rise to fatal levels for the tank occupants. If a stand is to be used, this should be solid, and able to support the weight of the aquarium once it is full. A layer of polystyrene will be necessary to compensate for any irregularities in the surface. A locality close to a power point is also to be recommended, to avoid trailing wires around the room.

The tank should just be washed out, to remove any dirt or slivers of glass that could be present within. The next step will be to fit an underground filter as required, covering the whole of the floor area, before adding gravel to a depth of 7·5 cm (3 ins) above. Thread the wires for electrical equipment through the hood, and set this in position in the tank, but do not connect up at this stage. Care must be taken when filling the tank to ensure that the gravel is not disturbed, so water from a clean bucket is usually poured onto a saucer placed on top of the gravel. A dechlorinator will need to be added to the water so that it is safe for the fish.

The actual chemistry of the water will vary according to the region concerned. Water from a limestone area, having passed over soluble rocks, will have minerals dissolved in it, causing it to be described as hard. By comparison, rainwater tends to be soft, not having come into contact with such rocks. Soft water tends to be acidic, having a pH value less than 7, whereas hard water is more usually alkaline, being above the neutral figure of 7. Domestic tap water tends to be about 7·2, although it is possible to get an accurate figure by testing a sample using a kit available from an aquarist store. In most cases, your local dealer will be able to advise on the prevailing water conditions in the area.

3 General Management

Fish are very easy to maintain, since there is a range of balanced prepared foods available to cater for their nutritional needs. These are in various forms, with pellets tending to be of most value for surface-feeders, since these float quite readily. Flaked food, which readily breaks into smaller particles is useful for fish that prefer to feed at the bottom of the aquarium, such as catfish. There are also diets available for specific groups of fish, including guppies and cichlids.

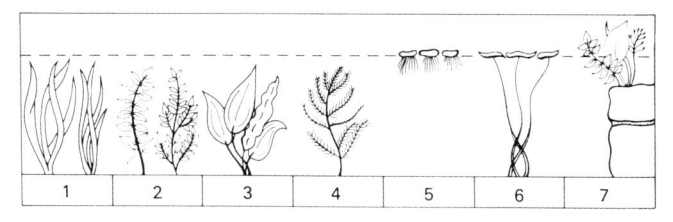

The main types of water plants:
1. With strap like leaves; 2. with coarse or mossy leaves; 3. with long stalks. 4. with feathery leaves; 5. floating plants; 6. rooted plants with floating leaves. 7. marsh plants.

In addition to these basic foods, other items such as freeze-dried tubifex worms can be offered. It is vital not to overfeed the fish however; in the wild, they feed almost constantly, so that several small offerings during the day are preferable to one large meal. Excess food simply pollutes the water, and burdens the filtration system, possibly to the fish's detriment. They should eat the quantity offered within minutes, otherwise it is too much. This fact is important to stress to anyone who looks after the fish in your absence, although it is possible to purchase special food blocks which will last for several days or so, making feeding unnecessary for this period.

Livefoods may be of aquatic origin, such as tubifex worms and daphnia, also known inaccurately as water fleas. Although popular with fish, livefood of this type is likely to introduce disease to an established aquarium. For this reason, many aquarists prefer to offer terrestrial livefoods, of which whiteworm is perhaps the most popular item. These small worms can be cultured in clean empty margarine tubs half-filled with damp peat. Soaked bread and milk buried below the surface acts as a food source for the worms, which can be purchased in the form of a starter culture. Kept at a temperature of about 20°C/68°F, it will take about a month for the culture to become well-established. Other tiny worms which can be kept in a similar way are microworms and grindal worms. Prior to feeding, the worms can be separated from the culture medium by immersing them in a saucer of water. For more vegetarian fish, extras such as chopped pieces of lettuce can be supplied, and may help to divert attention from plants in the aquarium.

Aquarium Maintenance

Once the aquarium is set up, time spent on maintenance will be negligible. It is likely that about eight hours light a day will be required, but if algal growth seems to be excessive, this should be reduced. The sides of the aquarium can be cleaned regularly from the outside by means of a magnetic cleaner, and siphons can be used occasionally to remove any accumulation of mulm on the gravel. Clearly, any dead fish should be removed at once, so as not to pollute the water, and similarly, dead plants must be taken out before they decompose.

About every month, the aquarium will benefit from a partial water change, with up to a quarter of the total volume being replaced by fresh clean water at the appropriate temperature. A dechlorinator will be useful at this stage, rather than having to leave the water to stand, allowing the chlorine to come out of solution. The gravel can be stirred over carefully, and the airstone checked for any blockages. If a box filter is used, the components will need to be changed probably about every month, although possibly more frequently if the fish are particularly messy.

Young fish have prodigious appetites, but it is important, especially if there is no filtration system, not to pollute the water with food. The best means of keeping the aquarium clean is to carry out regular partial water changes, until the fish are larger. Overcrowding must be avoided at all costs, and as the brood develop, so additional accommodation may become necessary. Surplus healthy stock may be sold to a local aquarist store, but any fish that are deformed should be painlessly killed, rather than simply flushed down a toilet. In the wild, such individuals would rapidly fall prey to other creatures, and they can alternatively be placed in a tank alongside predatory species, where they will have a speedy end. Indeed, it is no coincidence that egg-layers usually produce more eggs than the number of offspring resulting from live-bearers.

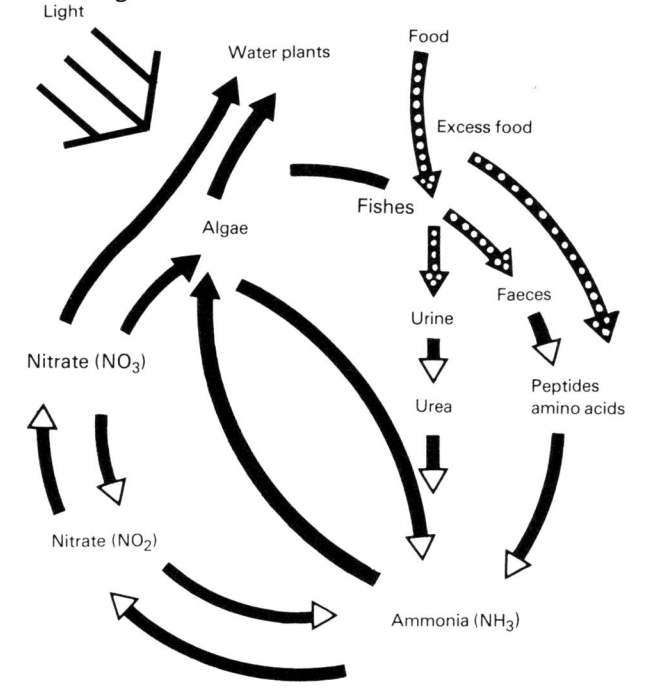

The nitrogen cycle:

The nitrogen cycle sees the degradation of toxic ammonia to less harmful compounds, notably nitrate which is used by algea and plants for their growth. Overfeeding fish will pollute the tank and overloads the cycle. The undergravel filter shows the cycle in operation.

4 **Breeding**

While fish will breed in a community aquarium, results will be better if additional accommodation is available. This applies especially in the case of egg-laying species which may otherwise consume their eggs, or fry that do hatch. With live-bearers, it is possible to accommodate the female in a breeding trap, which allows the young fish to escape out of reach of the female, but again, this is more satisfactorily accomplished in a spare tank.

Having recognised a pair of fish, the livefood content of their diet should be increased, to stimulate breeding behaviour, although this may not be necessary with live-bearers, which breed readily as a general rule. As a guide, females prior to spawning will become noticeably swollen, while males may grow brighter in overall coloration and will be seen driving the female, often nudging at her side. If a breeding tank is to be used, then the female should be transferred first, enabling her to settle down before the male is introduced. A simple plastic tank will suffice for the purpose, and to protect the eggs, the floor should be covered with a double layer of marbles. The eggs will slip down between the marbles out of reach of the adult fish, and as an added precaution, the water level should be kept low, so the eggs disappear rapidly. Another possible option is to drape fine netting over the sides of the tank, extending into the water. As the fish spawn, the eggs fall through beneath, onto the floor of the aquarium. In some instances, plants will need to be included in the spawning tank. Specific breeding requirements can be found under the individual species headings.

Rearing

Once the fry start to hatch, they will be nourished at first by the remains of their yolk sacs, until they actually start swimming, at which point the young fish will need food. Livebearers are generally larger than the offspring of egg-layers, and there are different formulated preparations available for these two groups, sold under the general description of fry foods. As the fish grow, they can be introduced to other items, including microworms. One of the most popular livefoods for young fish is brine shrimp, purchased in the form of eggs. It is preferable to obtain these without shells, as this improves their hatchability. The eggs can naturally survive for long periods out of water but need to be stored in dry surroundings. In order to hatch them successfully, a solution of sea-salt, mixed at the rate of 20 g to a litre of water ($\frac{1}{2}$ oz of salt to a pint of water) is to be recommended. The solution should be heated to 25°C/77°F, and about twelve hours after the eggs have been added, the young larval stage in the brine shrimp's life-cycle, known as the nauplii, will start to emerge. These should be sieved, rinsed thoroughly using dechlorinated water and then washed off into the tank containing the fry.

5 Health

Once the fish are established in their quarters, they are less likely to succumb to diseases, providing the tank is kept clean. For this reason, great caution is needed with new fish before introducing them to an established aquarium, and they must be quarantined in separate accommodation for three weeks. Care must be taken not to introduce disease by other means; nets for example can spread infections from one tank to another.

Proprietary remedies for most common fish ailments can be obtained without difficulty from an aquarist store, although in some cases, no effective treatment is possible and the fish should be painlessly destroyed.

Bacterial and Fungal Diseases

The most significant disease in this group is piscine tuberculosis, which is characterised by wasting of affected fish, and may be frequently linked with other signs, notably protrusion of the eyes, described as exophthalmos. There is no treatment for this infection, and mortality may be high, with the disease itself being confirmed by autopsy. Although this type of tuberculosis is not normally transmitted to humans, it can occasionally give rise to skin rashes. The wearing of gloves when cleaning

Fish diseases:
This diagram shows some of the common ailments which fish may succumb. A number are parasitic in origin and can be introduced to an aquarium by new fish, plants and live food.
Other ailments results from poor management.

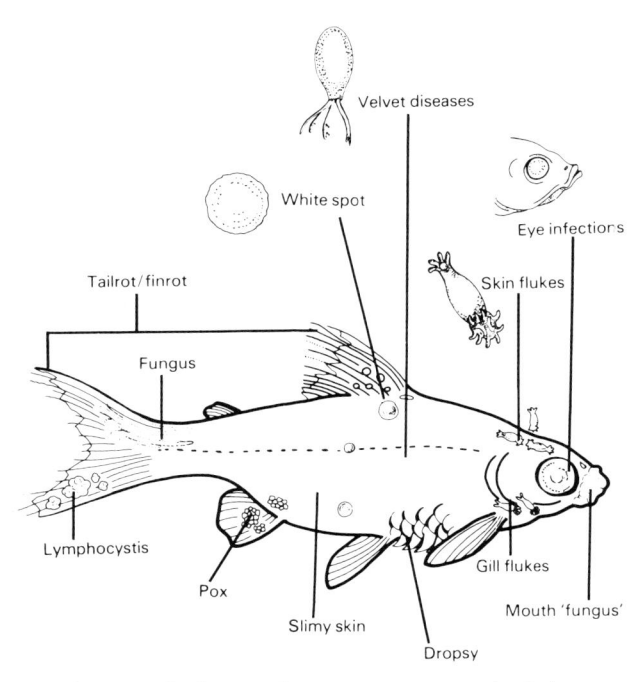

- Velvet diseases
- White spot
- Eye infections
- Tailrot/finrot
- Skin flukes
- Fungus
- Lymphocystis
- Pox
- Slimy skin
- Dropsy
- Gill flukes
- Mouth 'fungus'

out the tank is to be recommended in any event, since chemicals on the hands may poison the fish themselves. In cases of tuberculosis, the tank needs to be emptied completely, and treated with an iodine-based disinfectant, before being rinsed and refurbished.

Damage to the fins can also be traced to bacteria in many instances, and may be linked to environmental conditions such as dirty water. An underlying injury can also predispose to infections of this type, with fin-nipping being a particular cause. The fish may have to be watched closely to identify the culprit. If treated early, the fin may heal completely.

Swelling of the belly, resulting from an accumulation of fluid within the body cavity, described as dropsy, will cause the scales to protrude at an abnormal angle. Dropsy can prove an infectious complaint, so that fish showing such symptoms should be removed from a community tank. Treatment is again unlikely to be of value.

Another opportunist infection that will attack at sites of injury is the fungus *Saprolegnia*, which strikes weakened individuals in particular. It is evident as whitish streaks across the body surface, and can usually be treated satisfactorily with proprietary remedies. The so-called mouth fungus however results from a bacterial infection, and is not a fungal disorder, in spite of its name.

Parasites

These organisms frequently afflict aquarium fish, and probably the most common is 'white spot' or 'Ick', resulting from protozoal infection. This parasite has a complex life-cycle. As its name suggests, it is characterised by the appearance of white spots over the fish's body. These disappear and each cyst on the fish's body can generate as many as 1000 tomites, which are dependent on finding a host within a day or so if they are to survive. An epidemic can soon develop in an aquarium therefore, if just one fish is infected. Nevertheless, it is possible to destroy the parasite by using the appropriate medication over a period of time. The free-swimming tomite stage in the life-cycle is most vulnerable to the effects of treat-

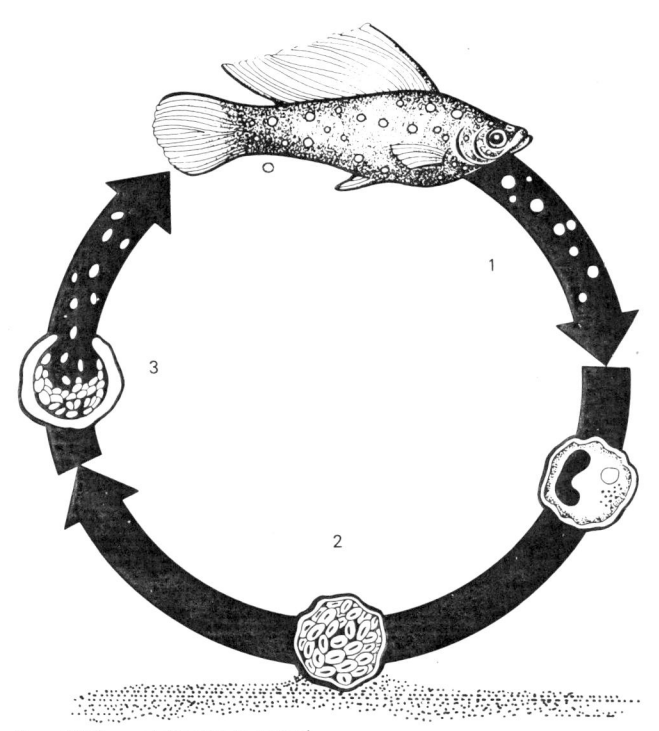

How White-spot disease is spread:
1. White spots are evident on the fish's body.
2. Parasites then spread forming cysts at the bottom of the aquarium.
3. These then give use to a free-swimming stage which infects the fish again.

ment. Other similar parasites may occasionally be encountered. *Oodinium* gives rise to the complaint known as Velvet Disease, because of the appearance of the body at the site of the infection, and will respond to similar treatment as recommended for white spot.

Skin flukes may occasionally be seen on the fish's body. Those affecting the gills are more serious, and harder to treat successfully. Internal parasites are generally less significant than the external counterparts, although the eye can be damaged irreparably in some instances by trematode larvae. The life-cycle of these parasites is sufficiently complex to ensure that it cannot be completed in the aquarium environment. In this instance, birds are the host of the adult trematode.

When using any treatments, always follow the instructions implicitly. It is preferable to use a plastic tank for isolation and treatment purposes, bearing in mind that many remedies are both inactivated by filtration over carbon, and may interfere with biological systems, especially in the case of antibiotics.

Sudden deaths in the aquarium may not in fact be due to any infectious cause, but result from poisoning. This is especially likely if a number of fish die in rapid succession. Many aerosols can prove deleterious to fishes' health, as will fumes including cigarette smoke that can also be introduced to the tank via the air pump. Pollution of the water itself may be responsible for deaths in some instances; new pipework can lead to excessive amounts of copper being present in solution, and for this reason, it is preferable to turn the tap on for several minutes to run off water which has been stationary in the pipework. The risk of chlorine being present in water has already been mentioned; this also will prove toxic to fish.

6 Shows and Societies

A surprisingly large number of local and national aquarist societies exist throughout the world. In addition, there are specialist groups catering for those with an interest in a particular group of fish, such a catfish. Societies also organise shows where fish are exhibited and judged competitively in some instances. Membership of such societies provides an easy means of meeting people with similar interests, and discussing problems, as well as keeping up to date with developments in the world of fish-keeping.

It is also well worth subscribing to the specialist magazines as an additional source of information. Many offer a free advisory service, as do some manufacturers, notably those who produce fish foods. Details in this instance are normally featured on the packaging of the products themselves. This particular book can only provide a brief introduction to the fascinating world of freshwater tropical fish-keeping. I hope it has been of some help and that your new hobby will give you hours of pleasure.